CHRISTIANITY

AND

ISLAM

HIGHLIGHTING
THEIR
SIMILARITIES:

THE ROAD TO PEACE

By

Mustafa El-Amin

Published by

EL-Amin Productions

P.O. Box 32148

Newark, NJ 07102

Copyright   2002

By Mustafa EL-Amin

All rights reserved

ISBN: 0-9638597-3-0

Table of Contents

DEDICATION

This book is dedicated to those courageous men and women who are working diligently on behalf of humanity and are doing their utmost to establish peace in the world.

I would like to thank all of those who influenced me in some way to write this book Those people are very special, especially my **grandfather** the late Reverend Allen Thomas of Sylvania, Georgia, Imam Warith Deen Mohammed, leader of the Muslim American Society, who has been diligently working to promote inter-faith dialogue, my two special life long friends, Umar Bey Ali and Ansari Nadir. Their friendship is more valuable than a ton of gold.

The words of encouragement and support given to me by brother Imams Yusuf Ali of Cleveland, Ohio, Mahdi Islam Muhammed of Hammond, Indiana and Bro. Elijah Muhammad of Newark, New Jersey are greatly appreciated and cherished. I would also like to thank Abdul Khabir Shamsid-Deen, of Elizabeth, New Jersey for his valuable input and advise.

Last, but not least I thank G'd for my wife and family.

INTRODUCTION

The universal teachings and principals of religion are needed more today than perhaps at any other time in history. The shock, fear and death that occurred on September 11, 2001 and its aftermath, has affected the soul, mind and spirit of millions of people.

Much has been said and written about the religion of Islam and its teachings. Many questions are being asked about this religion, which has a billion followers worldwide. The religion of Islam, as with the other Abrahamic faiths, promotes peace and harmony. The President and many other high level officials in the American government, as well as other world leaders have come out publicly and stated "Islam is a religion of peace."

The overwhelming majority of Muslims are peaceful law abiding citizens, as is the case with Christians and Jews. Each of these religions is connected in some way. Abraham is accepted as the father of the faithful of all three religions, Judaism, Christianity and Islam.

Our focus in this work is on the similarities that exist in the teachings of Christianity and Islam. The reason is that not enough people realize the closeness and the connection that these two great religions share. For example, both religions have a Holy book, teach a belief in G'd, the Creator, and in the existence of angels. Both teach that there is a Satan and that he was cast out from a heavenly state. Belief in the Day of Judgment, the Resurrection and the Hereafter are all-apart of the teachings of both these religions. Christians and Muslims are taught to fast, pray and give in charity; love and respect your fellow man. Their Holy books demand that they be truthful and honest, and to seek knowledge and wisdom. The followers of each of these religions are required to seek to be productive members of society.

In studying these two great religions, we also find that peace is an essential part of their doctrine. It is reported in the Holy Bible that Jesus Christ said, "Blessed are the peacemakers, for they shall be called the children of G'd." (Matthew 5: 9)ı. The Bible also informs us that Jesus greeted his followers, "peace be with you, my peace I leave with you." (John 14:27). Islam gives the same message of peace. One of the names of G'd in the Holy Qur'an is As- Salaam, The Peaceful, The Source of Peace   (59: 23) The words Islam and Muslim comes from an Arabic word which means peace, Salama. The Islamic greetings, As-Salaam Alaikum, means   "The Peace be unto you." Christianity and Islam encourage the practice of love.

So there are some very obvious similarities, that if, more of the leaders and followers in these religions would highlight, perhaps we would have a more peaceful world.

Concerning the relationship between Christianity and Islam, the Qur'an states: "Nearest in love to the Believers will you find are those who say 'We are Christians.' Because amongst them are men devoted to learning and men who are pious, and they are not arrogant. And when they hear what has been revealed to the messenger, you will see their eyes overflowing with tears on account of the truth that they recognize; they say 'Our Lord! We believe, so write us down with the witnesses." (5: 85,86)

In addressing the future relationship of Christians and Muslims, it is reported that Muhammad The Prophet said to his followers about 1400 years ago, "in the future you will see I and Christ Jesus together." Imam Warith Deen Mohammed, leader of the Muslim American Society, explained in a Jummah lecture, that what is meant by Prophet Muhammad's (pub) statement that he and Christ Jesus will be together is, "That those people who were in opposition to Islam, to the Qur'an and Muhammad, from

Christianity, would one day (in the future) come to see Christ Jesus, peace be upon him, in agreement with Muhammad."(See, Muslim Journal, Vol. 27 No. 28, April 19, 2002). In further making the point that these two religions have a close relationship, let me present a brief but very important event in history.

A Christian King: A True Friend to Muslims

According to Islamic history, during the seventh century, shortly after Muhammad received the revelation of the Qur'an, their own Arab people persecuted him and his followers. The torture and persecution became so severe until he sent some of his followers to Abyssinia (now called Ethiopia) a Christian country, to escape the persecution. The king of Abyssinia was a devout Christian, a fair and just King. He allowed the Muslims to enter his country under his protection. It is reported that the persecutors tried to persuade the King not to give the Muslims asylum and to turn the Muslims over to them. The King rejected them each time.

The persecutors, in an effort to persuade the King, told him that the Muslims practiced a religion that taught against Jesus and the Christian Faith. The King then asked the Muslims to tell him something of their religion and what it says about Jesus Christ. They replied by quoting some verses from the Qur'an concerning Jesus. After hearing what the Qur'an says, it is reported that the King took a stick and drew a line in the sand, and then said to the Muslims "your religion and my religion are only as distant as this line." He continued to grant the Muslims protection and asylum. The persecutors were made to leave.

This event clearly reflects true religious brotherhood that goes beyond labels. People of faith form one brotherhood that is concerned with pleasing G'd and serving humanity. It is obvious that over time misunderstanding, greed, deception and war created a vast rift between these two great Faiths. However, the pure essence in the scriptures of the Abrahamic Faiths remained intact. The continuity of the divine revelation continued to exist. Therefore, if we were to examine the Holy Bible and the Holy Qur'an, with pure intentions and an open mind, we will see that they are not separate, but in fact a continuation of the Word of G'd that has been unfolding from the beginning of time. We hope to show this by using verses that carry a similar message that is obvious. We will also show this by presenting Biblical and Qur'anic references that alludes to the similarities and the continuity of divine revelation. To accomplish this I have devoted an entire chapter entitled: **Connecting the Knowledge**

My purpose in writing this book is not only to highlight the similarities between Christianity and Islam, but also to show the oneness and continuity of the scriptures. In so doing, perhaps I will help the followers of these two great religions come to understand and better appreciate one another. If that happens, we would have taken a giant step along the road to peace.

In an effort to simplify this work and to give the reader an easier way of comparing the teachings of both holy books, Bible and Qur'an, I decided to present various aspects of the teachings of both religions as they are given in the Bible and the Qur'an using direct quotes. The reader should also take note that the word God in this book is spelled G'd, out of respect for the sacredness of the name.

CHAPTER 1

THE BELIEF IN G'D

Belief in G'd, as the Creator is essential to all religions, especially the Abrahamic Faiths. Christianity and Islam share a common belief in G'd as the Creator, All Powerful, All Knowing and Merciful. Although their expressions and terminology may differ, both religions adhere to the belief in a Power that is greater than man and the universe. They teach that G'd created man, fashioned and designed this vast universe, and that He knows the beginning and the end. Both of these religions share the belief and practice of prayer, charity and fasting, to name a few. Concerning prayer, it is interesting to note that both of these religions have an "often- said" prayer. Christianity has the "Lord's Prayer" and Islam has "The Opening Prayer", called Al- Fatiha, which also means "The Victory." It consists of seven verses, which some, say alludes to the opening of the "Book of Seven Seals" that is mentioned in the Bible. (Revelation 5: 1-4 and Isaiah 29: 11, 12, 18)

Let us look more closely at what the Bible and the Qur'an says about belief in G'd, angels, prayer, charity, fasting and the Day of Judgment.

Christianity: What It Says About One G'd

The Bible says:"The Lord thy G'd is one Lord, and thou shalt love the Lord thy G'd with all thine heart and with all thy soul and all thy might." (Deut. 6:4) The Holy Bible also says that Jesus said to one of the scribes "The first of all the commandments is, Hear, O Israel; The Lord our G'd is one Lord" The Bible continues to say, "And the scribe said unto him (Jesus), well Master, thou hast said the truth: for there is one G'd, and there is none other but He" (Mark 12:29, 32) The Bible informs us that; In the beginning G'd created the heaven and the earth...And G'd said "let there be light and there was light."

Islam: What It Says About One G'd

The Qur'an says: "Say, Your G'd is one G'd; so those who do not believe in the hereafter, their hearts are ignorant and they are arrogant."(16:22) In a chapter entitled: Iron, it says, "Whatever is in the heavens and the earth declares the glory of Allah (G'd), and He is the Mighty, the Wise. His is the kingdom of the heavens and the earth; He gives life and causes death; and He has power over all things. He is the First and the Last and the Ascendant (over all) and the Knower of hidden things, and He has knowledge of every thing. He it is Who created the heavens and the earth in six periods, and He is firm in power. He knows that which goes deep down into the earth and that which comes forth out of it, and that which comes down from heaven and that which goes up into it, and He is with you wherever you are, and G'd sees all that you do. His is the kingdom of the heavens and the earth; and to Allah (G'd) is the return of all affairs. He causes the night to enter in upon the day, and causes the day to enter in upon the night, and He has full knowledge of what is in the hearts (of all people)." (57: 1-6)

Christianity: The Importance of Prayer

The Bible informs us that Jesus said, "And all things, whatsoever ye shall ask in prayer, believing, ye shall receive." (Matthew 21: 22) The Bible also says: "And the prayer of faith shall save the sick, and the Lord shall raise him up, and if he committed sins, they shall be forgiven him." (James 5: 15) The Bible says that Peter said; "But the end of all things is at hand: be ye therefore sober and watch unto prayer."(1 Peter 4: 7) We are also told in the Bible that Jesus taught his followers "The Lord's Prayer." Now let us look at the "Lord's Prayer."

6

The Lord's Prayer

Our Father which art in heaven, Hallowed be thy name. Thy Kingdom come. Thy will be done in earth, as it is in heaven. Give us this day our daily bread. And forgive us our debts, as we forgive our debtors. And lead us not into temptation, but deliver us from evil: For thine is the kingdom, and the power, and the glory, forever. Amen

The Bible tells us that Jesus warned his followers concerning their intentions while performing prayer. He said: "And when thou prayest, thou shalt not be as the hypocrites are: for they love to pray standing in the synagogues and in the corners of the streets, that they may be seen of men. Verily I say onto you, they have their reward."(Matthew 6:5)

Islam: The Importance of Prayer

The Qur'an says, "And keep up prayer and pay the poor-rate and whatever good you send before for yourselves, you shall find it with G'd; surely G'd sees what you do. (2:110) And keep up prayer in the two parts of the day and in the first hours of the night; surely good deeds take away evil deeds; this is a reminder to the mindful. (11:114) Keep up prayer from the declining of the sun till the darkness of the night, and the morning recitation; surely the morning recitation is witnessed. (17:78) Attend constantly to prayers and to the middle prayer and stand up truly obedient to G'd. (2: 238) This is the Book (Qur'an), there is no doubt in it, is a guide to those who are regardful. Those who believe in the unseen and keep up prayer and spend out of what We have given them" (2: 2-3)

"Have you considered him who calls the Judgment a lie? That is the one who treats the orphan with harshness, and does not urge the feeding of the poor. So woe to the praying ones, who are unmindful of their prayers, who (wish) to be seen, and withhold the basic things of life." (107: 1-7)

7

Al-Fatiha, The Opening

1. With G'd's Name The Merciful Benefactor, The Merciful Redeemer.

2. All praise is due to G'd, The Lord of all the worlds. (and systems of knowledge)

3. The Merciful Benefactor, The Merciful Redeemer.

4. Master of the Day of Judgment

5. You do we worship and You do we seek for assistance.

6. Guide us on the straight path.

7. The path of those upon whom You have bestowed Your favor; not of those upon whom Your wrath is brought down, nor of those who go astray.

Christianity: The Importance of Charity

The Bible says, "And above all things have fervent charity among yourselves: For charity shall cover the multitude of sins" (1 Peter 4:8). It also says: "And now abideth faith, hope charity, these three; but the greatest of these, charity (1 Corinthians 13:13)

Islam: The Importance of Charity

The Qur'an says; " So be regardful of G'd, listen and obey; and spend in charity for the benefit of your own souls and those saved from the covetousness of their own souls; they are the ones that achieve prosperity". (64:16) The Qur'an also states; "They ask you (Muhammad, The Prophet, prayers and peace be upon him), what they should spend in (charity). Say: what ever you spend that is good, is for parents and kindred and orphans and those in want and for wayfarers. And whatever you do that is good, G'd knows it well" (2: 215) We also find in the Qur'an a parable of those who give in charity. It says:

"The parable of those who spend their wealth in the way of G'd is as that of a grain of corn: it growth seven ears, and each ear hath a hundred grains. G'd giveth manifold increase to whom He pleases: And G'd careth for all and He knowth all things". The Qur'an continues in another place with a caution to the believers. It states: "O you who believe! Cancel not your charity by reminders of your generosity or by harm, like those who spend their wealth to be seen of men, but believe neither in G'd nor in the Last Day..." (2:261 and 264)

Christianity: Fasting

The Bible says that Jesus fasted for forty days and forty nights. It states: "Then was Jesus led up of the Spirit into the wilderness to be tried by the devil. And when he had fasted forty days and forty nights, he was afterward an hungered." (Matthew 4:1,2)

The Bible also says that Jesus told his followers, "When thou fastest, anoint thine head, and wash thy face."(Matthew 6:17)

Islam: Fasting

The Qur'an says: "O You who believe, Fasting is prescribed to you as it was prescribed to those before you, that you may be regardful. (Fasting) for a fixed number of days; But if any of you is ill or on a journey, the prescribed number (should be made up) from days later. For those who can do it (having hardship), is a ransom, the feeding of one that is indigent. But he that will give more, of his own free will, it is better for him. And it is better for you that you fast, if you but knew...Ramadan is the (month) in which the

Qur'an was sent down, as a guide to mankind, also clear (signs) for guidance and judgment; so every one of you who is present (not traveling) during that month should spend it in fasting…"(2: 183)

Chapter Summary

Belief in G'd is the cornerstone of both these religions. They both require their adherents to have discipline and to fast seeking G'd's pleasure. This chapter shows the similarities in Christianity and Islam in a very important way. Belief in G'd, prayer fasting and giving charity are some of the essentials in both religions.

CHAPTER 2

BELIEF IN ANGELS AND THE DAY OF JUDGMENT

The Bible and the Qur'an advances the idea of the existence of spiritual beings called angels. Christianity and Islam require their adherents to believe in angels as messengers and helpers of mankind in this world. Both of these religions also teach that angels will play a major role on the "Day of Judgment", and in the after life.

In further presenting the similarities between Christianity and Islam, we list here verses from the Bible and the Qur'an that clearly shows that Christians and Muslims are taught that angels do exist and that they must believe that.

Christianity: Gabriel and Michael

The Bible says: " And Zechariahs said unto the angel, whereby shall I know this, for I am an old man, and my wife well stricken in years, And the angel answering said unto him, I am Gabriel that stand in the presence of G'd; and am sent to speak unto thee and to shew thee these glad tidings" (Luke 1: 18, 19)

"Yea, while I was speaking in prayer, even the man Gabriel whom I had seen in the vision at the beginning, being caused to fly swiftly, touched me about the time of the evening oblation. And he informed me, and talked with me and said, O Daniel, I am now come forth to give thee skill and understanding." (Daniel 9:21-22)

"Yet Michael the archangel when contending with the devil, he disputed about the body of Moses..." (Jude 9)

Islam: Gabriel (Jibreel) and Michael (Meekal)

The Qur'an says; "Whoever is an enemy of G'd and His angels and His messengers and Gabriel and Michael, so surely G'd is the enemy of the unbelievers." (2:98)

"Say: Whoever is the enemy of Gabriel, for surely he revealed it (The Qur'an) to your (Muhammad, the prophet, pbuh) heart by G'd's permission, verifying that which is before it and guidance and good news for the believers." (2: 97)

"Relate in the Book, Mary, when she withdrew from her family to a place in the East. She placed a screen (to hide herself) from them; Then We sent to her Our angel, and he appeared before her as a man in all respects." (19: 16-17)

Christianity: The Day of Judgment

The Bible says that there is a day coming when we will all be judged by G'd for our deeds in this life. It states: "The heavens and the earth which are now …kept in store, reserved unto fire against the day of judgment and perdition of ungodly men."

"The day of the Lord will come as a thief in the night; in the which the heavens shall pass away with a great noise, and the elements shall melt with fervent heat, the earth also and the works that are therein shall be burned up." (II Peter 3: 7-10)

"In a moment, **in the twinkling of an eye, at** the last trump: For the trumpet shall sound, and the dead shall be raised incorruptible, and we shall be changed." (I Corinthians 15:52)

John the revelator writes: "And I saw the dead, small and great, stand before G'd; and the books were opened: And another book was opened, which is the book of life: and the dead were judged out of those things which were written in the books, according to their work. And the sea gave up the dead, which were in it; and death and hell delivered up the dead, which were in them: and they were judged every man according to their works. And death and hell were cast into the lake of fire. This is the second death. And whosoever was not found written in the book of life was cast into the lake of fire. And I saw a new heaven and a new earth: for the first heaven and the first earth were passed away; and there was no more sea." (Revelation; 20:12-15 and 21:1)

"Be not ignorant of this one thing, that one day is with the Lord as a thousand years and a thousand years as one day." (II Peter 3: 8)

Islam: The Day of Judgment

The Qur'an, like the Bible says that there will be a new creation after the Day of Judgment. "The Day that We roll up the heavens like a scroll rolled up for a book; Even as We produced the first creation, so shall We produce a new one. A promise We have undertaken: Truly shall We fulfill it. Before this we wrote in the Psalms, after the Message (to Moses): "My servants, the righteous shall inherit the earth." (21:104,105)

The Qur'an also says: "They ask you (Muhammad) about the hour, when will it be? Say: "The knowledge of it is only with my Lord; none but He shall manifest it at its time, It will be momentous in the heavens and the earth. It will only come on you suddenly, they ask you as if you were seeking it. Say, Its knowledge is only with Allah, G'd, but most people do not know" (7: 187)

"And to G'd belongs the unseen of the heavens and the earth, and the matter of the hour is but **as the twinkling of an eye** or it is closer still. Surely G'd has power over all things." (16: 77)

"And the trumpet shall be blown, so all those that are in the heavens and all those that are in the earth shall swoon, except such as G'd pleases; then it shall be blown again, then lo! They shall stand up waiting. And the earth shall beam with the light of its Lord, and the Book shall be laid down, and the prophets and the witnesses shall be brought up and judgment shall be given between them with justice, and they shall not be dealt with unjustly. And every soul shall be paid back fully what it has done. And He (G'd) knows best what they do." (39: 68-70)

The Qur'an, like the Bible also says:" Verily a day in the sight of your Lord is like a thousand years of your counting." (22:47)

Chapter Summary

We cannot explain everything that happens in our life. There are powers that impact on our lives from places we know not. This chapter verifies that these two Abrahamic Faiths teach that G'd has assigned angels to assist us in our lives in some way. The quotes from the Holy Bible and the Holy Qur'an informs us that these two religions recognizes the fact that G'd sends Gabriel as the angel to bring revelation. This chapter demonstrates clearly that both religions teach that there is a final day called the Day of Judgment and that it will come in "the twinkling of an eye." And that a day with the Lord is as a thousand years.

CHAPTER 3

THE CREATION OF MAN

Christianity and Islam teach that the human being was created by G'd The Creator and entrusted with power and authority in this universe. The Bible and the Qur'an gives similar explanations of the creation of Adam, the human being. Both books make it very clear that Almighty G'd created the human being to walk in the light of faith, knowledge and wisdom, and to be industrious. These two Abrahamic Faiths inform us that the Creator, in His mercy, gave the human being something of His own spirit.

Christianity: Adam's Creation

The Holy Bible says: "There went up a mist from the earth and watered the whole face of the ground. And the Lord God formed man of the dust of the ground and **breathed** into his nostrils the breath of life and he became a living soul."(Genesis 2:6-7)

Islam: Adam's Creation

The Qur'an says: "It is He Who has created man from water"(25:54) The Qur'an also says "He it is Who created you from clay" (6:2) It also says in (15:26, 28-29) "We created man from sounding clay, from mud fashioned into shape...Behold! Your Lord said to the angels, I am creating a mortal from mud moulded into shape...When I have fashioned him and **breathed** into him of My spirit, fall you down in obeisance to him"

Christianity: Man is made the Ruler in Creation

The Bible says: "And G'd said Let Us make man in Our image, after Our likeness: And let them have dominion over the fish of the sea and over the fowl of the air, and over the cattle and over all the earth, and over every creeping thing that creepeth upon the earth." (Gen 1: 26)

Islam: Man is made the Ruler in Creation

The Qur'an says: "And the cattle He has created for you ...and horses, mules and donkeys (He created for you). He has made subject to you the night and the day, the sun and the moon and the stars are in subjection to you by His command: Verily in this are signs for men who reason. It is He Who has made subject to you the sea, that you may eat thereof flesh that is fresh and tender, and that you may extract there from ornaments to wear ..."(16: 5,8,12,14)

Christianity: Adam named the Creation

The Bible says: "And out of the ground the Lord G'd formed every beast of the field and every fowl of the air, and brought them unto Adam to see what he would call them: And whatsoever Adam called every living creature, that was the name thereof...And Adam gave names to all cattle and to the fowl of the air and to every beast of the field." (Genesis 2:19-20)

Islam: Adam named the Creation

The Qur'an says: "And He taught Adam the names (nature) of all things, then He placed them before the angels and said tell Me the names (nature) of these if you are right.... He said "O Adam! Tell them their names (nature)" When Adam had told them, G'd said, "Did not I tell you that I know the secrets of heaven and earth and I know what you reveal and what you conceal." (2: 31, 33)

Christianity: The Fall of Man: Tricked by Satan

The Bible says: "Now the serpent was more subtle than any beast of the field which the Lord G'd had made. And he said unto the woman, Yea, has G'd said, you shall not eat of every tree of the garden. And the woman said unto the serpent, we may eat of the fruit of the trees of the garden: But of the fruit of the tree which is in the midst of the garden, G'd has said you shall not eat of it, neither shall you touch it, lest you die.

And the serpent said unto the woman, you shall not surely die: For G'd do know that in the day you eat thereof, then your eyes shall be opened and you shall be as gods, knowing good and evil.

The Lord G'd sent him forth from the garden of Eden, to till the ground from which he was taken." (Genesis 3: 1-5, 23, 24)

Islam: The Fall of Man: Tricked by Satan

The Qur'an says: "O Adam dwell you and your wife in the garden and enjoy as you wish: But approach not this tree or you run into harm and transgression. Then Satan began to whisper suggestions to them bringing openly before their minds all their shame that was hidden from them (before). He said "Your Lord only forbade you this tree lest you should become angels or such beings as live forever.

And he swore to them both that he was their sincere adviser. So by deceit he brought about their fall...They said "Our Lord we have wronged our own souls: If You forgive us not and bestow not upon us your mercy, we shall certainly be lost.

Allah said " get you down from here with enmity between yourselves, on earth will be your dwelling place and your means of livelihood, for a time.

17

He said: "Therein shall you live and therein shall you die, but from it shall you be taken out" (7:19-25)

Chapter Summary

G'd entrusted the human being with leadership in this creation. We are created in honor and nobility. The story of the creation of Adam is a very beautiful one. When we read it from both the Bible and the Qur'an the consistence of the scriptures becomes very evident. Both religions help us to understand that Satan got busy right away trying to prove the human being unworthy of the great responsibility that G'd entrusted him with.

CHAPTER 4

ABRAHAM: FATHER OF THE FAITHFUL

Jews, Christians and Muslims consider Abraham the father of the faithful; they all consider themselves the "Children of Abraham." He was a man of great faith, devotion and reasoning. The Bible and the Qur'an inform us that Abraham received a covenant from G'd and that he fulfilled all of his obligations. Both books also inform us that Abraham was willing to sacrifice his son in obedience to G'd.

We are also told in the Bible and Qur'an that Abraham is called "The Friend of G'd" and that he was true and upright.

Christianity: Abraham: The Friend of G'd

The Bible says "And the Scripture was fulfilled which says, Abraham believed G'd and it was given to him for righteousness. And he was called the friend of G'd."(James 2:23)

Islam: Abraham: The Friend of G'd

"Who can be better in religion than one who submits his whole self to G'd, does good and follows the way of Abraham, The true in Faith? For G'd did take Abraham for a friend." (4:125)

Christianity: Abraham Fulfilled His Obligations

The Bible says G'd said: "And I will make thy seed to multiply as the stars of heaven, and will give unto thy seed all these countries; and in thy seed shall all the nations of the earth be blessed; Because that Abraham obeyed my voice and kept my charge, my commandments, my statutes, and my laws" (Genesis 26; 4,5).

Islam: Abraham Fulfilled His Obligations

The Qur'an says "And remember that Abraham was tried by his Lord with certain commands, which he fulfilled. He (G'd) said "I will make you an Imam to all mankind:" He (Abraham) asked. "And also from my offspring?" He (G'd) answered, "but my promise is not within the reach of the evil doers" (2:124)

Christianity: The Promise to Abraham

The Bible says: "And I G'd will make of thee a great nation, and I will bless thee and make thy name great, and thou shalt be a blessing. And I will bless them that bless you and cruse them that curseth you: And in thee shall all families of the earth be blessed". (Genesis 12:2-3)

Islam: The Promise to Abraham

The Qur'an says: He (G'd) said, "I will make you an Imam (leader) to all mankind...Abraham was a (model community (or nation), devoutly obedient to G'd, true in faith, and he joined not g'ds with G'd: He showed his gratitude for the favors of G'd, who chose him and guided him to a straight way. And We gave him good in this world, and he will be in the hereafter in the ranks of the righteous. So We have taught the inspired (message), Follow the Millah (way) of Abraham, the true in faith. And he enjoined not g'ds with G'd". (2:124 and 16:120-125)

The Qur'an also states: " And who turns away from the path of Abraham, except such as degrade their souls with folly? Him we chose and rendered pure in this world: And he will be in the hereafter in the ranks of the righteous."(2:130)

Christianity: Abraham's Son, Ishmael

The Bible says: And the angel of the Lord said unto her (Hagar), "I will multiply thy seed exceedingly, that it shall not be numbered for multitude. And the angel of the lord said unto her, behold, thou art with child, and shall bear a son, and shalt call his name Ishmael; because the Lord hath heard your affliction." (Genesis 16:10-11)

The Bible also tells us, that while Hagar and her son, Ishmael, were in the desert, G'd said to Hagar, "Arise, lift up the baby and hold him in thine hand, for I will make him, a great nation." (Gen.21:18)

Islam: Abraham's Son, Ishmael

The Qur'an says: "Also mention in the Book: (the story of) Ishmael: He was true to what he promised and he was a messenger, a prophet. (19:54) Abraham prayed: "Praise be to G'd, Who hath granted unto me in old age, Ismail and Ishaq (Ishmael and Isaac) for truly my Lord is He, the Hearer of prayer." (14:39)

Christianity: Concerning Isaac's Birth

The Bible explains the birth of Isaac as follows: "And the Lord appeared unto him (Abraham) in the plains of Mamre: and he (Abraham) sat in the tent door in the heat of the day. And he lift up his eyes and looked, and lo three men stood by him: and when he saw them he ran to meet them from the tent door, and bowed himself toward the ground, and said "my Lord, if now I have found favor in thy sight, pass not away, I pray thee, from thy servant: Let a little water, I pray you, be fetched and wash your feet, and rest yourselves under the tree...

And they said where is Sarah, thy wife?" And he said, "behold in the tent, and he said, I will certainly return unto thee according to the time of life, and lo, Sarah, thy

wife shall have a son. And Sarah heard it in the tent door, which was behind him. Now Abraham and Sarah were old and well stricken in old age; and it ceased to be with Sarah after the manner of women. Therefore Sarah laughed within herself, saying, after I am waxed old shall I have pleasure, my lord being old also? And the Lord said unto Abraham, wherefore did Sarah laugh, saying shall I of a surety bear a child, which is old? Is anything to hard for the Lord? At the time appointed I will return unto thee, according to the time of life, and Sarah shall have a son."
(Genesis 18: 1-4 and 9-14)

Islam: Concerning Isaac's Birth

The Qur'an states: "Has the story reached you of the honored guest of Abraham? Behold, they entered his presence and said: "Peace". He said, "Peace"! (He thought to himself) "unusual people". Then he turned quickly to his household, brought out a fatted calf, and placed it before them. He said, "Will you not eat" He conceived a fear of them. They said, "Fear not". And they gave him good news of a son, endowed with knowledge. But his wife came forward laughing aloud: she hit her forehead and said "a barren old woman!" They said "even so hast your Lord spoken: And He is full of wisdom and knowledge".
(51:24-30)

Christianity: Abraham's Sacrifice

According to the Holy Bible: "It came to pass after all these things, that G'd did tempt Abraham, and said unto him "Abraham", And he said: " Behold, here I am." And he (G'd) said, "Take now thy son, thine only son, Isaac, whom thou lovest and get thee into the land of Moriah, and offer him there for a burnt offering upon one of the mountains which I will tell thee of...And they came to the place which G'd had told him of; and Abraham built an altar there, and laid the wood in order, and bound Isaac, his son, and laid him on the altar, upon the wood. And Abraham stretched forth his hand, and took the knife to slay his son. And the angel of the Lord called unto him out of heaven, and said, "Abraham, Abraham," And he said: "here am I", and he (the angel) said, lay not thine hand upon the lad (baby), neither do thou anything unto him. For now I know that thou fearest G'd, seeing thou hast not withheld thy son, thine only son from me.

And Abraham lifted up his eyes, and looked and behold behind him a ram caught in a thicket, by his horns and Abraham went and took the ram and offered him up for a burnt offering in the stead of his son."
(Genesis 22: 1-2, 9-13)

Islam: Abraham's Sacrifice

According to the Qur'an: "Then when (the son) reached the age of work with him. He said: "O my son! I see in a vision that I offer you in sacrifice: Now see what is your view. (The son) said: O my father! Do as thou art commanded. You will find me if G'd so wills, one practicing patience and constancy. So when they had both submitted their wills (to G'd) and he had laid prostate on his forehead (for sacrifice), We called out to him, " O Abraham! You have already fulfilled the vision!" Thus indeed do We reward those who do right. For this was obviously a trial- and We ransomed him with a mighty sacrifice.

And We left (this blessing) for him among generations (to come) in later times. "Peace and salutation to Abraham"! Thus indeed do We reward those who do right. For he was one of Our believing servants". (37: 102-111)

Chapter Summary

Abraham holds a special place in the religions of Judaism, Christianity and Islam. The verses quoted above only gives us a small idea of the role of Abraham in these religions. However, those verses do a big job in showing the similarities in the teachings of Christianity and Islam concerning Abraham. This chapter also informs us of the fact that Abraham and his sons are mentioned in the Qur'an.

CHAPTER 5

JACOB AND THE TRIBES

The Bible and the Qur'an inform us of Jacob and his twelve sons. Although the Qur'an doesn't present the twelve tribes with the details that the Bible does, it makes it very clear that Muslims must believe in and accept that Jacob had twelve sons who became the twelve tribes. In this chapter we won't attempt to discuss the details, we will only list the names of the tribes under Christianity and quote a few verses under Islam.

Christianity: The Names of the Twelve Tribes

According to the Bible Jacob became Israel and he had twelve sons, which are the twelve tribes. The names of the twelve tribes are:

1. Reuben

2. Simeon

3. Levi

4. Judah

5. Issachar

6. Zebulun

7. Joseph

8. Benjamin

9. Dan

10. Naphtali

11. Gad

12. Asher

Islam: The Twelve Tribes

The Qur'an makes it clear that those who practice the Islamic Faith should say:

"We believe in Allah (G'd) and that which had been revealed to us and that which was revealed to Abraham and Ismail and Isaac and Jacob and the **Tribes** and that which was given to Moses and Jesus and that which was given to the prophets from their Lord, we do not make any distinction between any of them, and to Him do we submit."

The Qur'an also says "Nay! Were you witnesses when death visited Jacob, when he said to his sons; what will you worship after me? They said, we will worship your G'd and the G'd of your father, Abraham and Ismael and Isaac; One G'd only, and to Him do we submit" (2: 136,133)

Chapter Summary

Jacob and his twelve sons, who became the twelve tribes, are very important in the Abrahamic Faiths. This chapter underscores the fact that Jacob is a righteous prophet and messenger of G'd and that Muslims recognize, accept and believe in all the prophets mentioned in the Bible. This chapter like the others, verify that there are many similarities between Christianity and Islam.

CHAPTER 6

THE STORY OF JOSEPH

We find in both religions a detailed account of Joseph, the son of Jacob. The conspiracy by his brothers to separate him from their father, Jacob and his ultimate victory and re-union with his father and family, seems to hold a special place in both of these Faiths. The Qur'an has an entire chapter devoted to the story of Joseph. That chapter is entitled, Yusuf (Joseph).

Let us look at some aspects of the story of Joseph as they are presented in the Bible and the Qur'an.

Christianity: Joseph's Vision

The Bible states: "And he (Joseph) dreamed another dream, and told it to his brethren and said, behold, I have dreamed a dream more; and behold, the sun and the moon and the eleven stars made obeisance to me. And his brethren envied him; but his father observed the saying."
(Genesis 37:9-11)

Islam: Joseph's Vision

The Qur'an states: "When Yusuf (Joseph) said to his father, O my father! Surely I saw eleven stars and the sun and the moon, I saw them making obeisance to me. He (Jacob) said, "O my son, do not relate your vision to your brothers, lest they devise a plot against you. Surely the Shaitan (Satan) is an open enemy to man" (12:4-5)

Christianity: Joseph's Brothers' Conspire Against Him

The Bible says: "And when they saw him afar off, even before he came near unto them, they conspired against him to slay him. And they said one to another, behold, this dreamer cometh. Come now therefore and let us slay him and cast him into some pit and we will say some evil beast hath devoured him and we shall see what will become of his dreams. And Reuben heard it, and he delivered him out of their hands and said, let us not kill him. And Reuben said unto them, shed no blood, but cast him into this pit that is in the wilderness, and lay no hand upon him, that he might rid him out of their hands to deliver him to his father again. And they took him and cast him into a pit, and the pit was empty. There was no water in it". (Geneses 37: 18-22,24)

Islam: Joseph's Brothers' Conspire Against Him.

The Qur'an says: "When they (his brothers) said: Certainly Joseph and his brother (Benjamin) are dearer to our father than we, though we are a (stronger) company. Most surely our father is in manifest error. Slay Joseph or cast him into some land, so that your father's regard may be exclusively for you, and after that you may be a righteous people. A speaker from among them said: Do not slay Yusuf (Joseph) and cast him down into the bottom of the pit, if you must do (it) some of the travelers may pick him up". (12:8-10)

Christianity: Joseph Taken Into Egypt

The Bible states: "Then there passed by Midianites merchantmen; and they drew and lifted up Joseph out of the pit and sold Joseph to the Ishmeelites for twenty pieces of silver. And they brought Joseph into Egypt. And the Midianites sold him into Egypt unto Potiphar, an officer of Pharaoh's and captain of the guard"(Genesis 37:28-36)

Islam: Joseph Taken Into Egypt

The Qur'an states: "And there came travelers and they sent their water-drawer and he let down his bucket. He said: "O good news! this is a youth, and they concealed him as an article of merchandise and Allah (G'd) knew what they did. And they sold him for a small price, a few pieces of silver, and they showed no desire for him." (12:19-20)

Christianity: Joseph Cast Into Prison

The Bible says: "And Joseph's master took him and put him into the prison, a place where the king's prisoners' were bound. And he (Joseph) was there in the prison. But the Lord was with Joseph and shewed him mercy, and gave him favor in the sight of the keeper of the prison.

And Pharaoh was worth against two of his officers, against the chief butler and against the chief of the bakers. And he put them in a ward in the house of the captain of the guard, into the prison, the place where Joseph was bound. And the captain of the guard charged Joseph with them, and he served them: and they continued a season in ward (Genesis 39:20-21 and 40:2-4)

Islam: Joseph Cast Into Prison

The Qur'an says "When Joseph attained his full manhood, We gave him power and knowledge: thus do We reward those who do right. Then it occurred to the men after they had seen the signs, to imprison him for a time."

"O my two companions of the prison! As to one of you, he will pour out the wine for his lord to drink. As for the other, he will hang from the cross and the birds will eat from off his head. This has been decreed that matter whereof you two do enquire" – said Joseph (12:22,35, 41)

Joseph made a Ruler in Egypt and Placed Over the Store-House

After the king of Egypt requested that Joseph be brought up from prison in order to interpret the kings dreams, and he did so, correctly, Joseph was made a ruler in Egypt and placed over the house where the king stored the grain. The religions of Christianity and Islam give an account of the story in a way that is thought provoking and interesting.

Christianity: Joseph Is Made A Ruler

The Bible says: And Pharaoh said unto Joseph, "Forasmuch as G'd hath shewed thee all this, there is none so discreet and wise as thou art. Thou shalt be over my house and according unto thy word shall all my people be ruled. Only in the throne will I be greater than thou"
(Genesis 41:39-40)

Islam: Joseph Is Made A Ruler

The Qur'an says: "He (Joseph) said, set me over the store-house of the land: I will indeed guard them as one that knows (their importance). Thus did We give established power to Joseph in the land to take possession therein as, when or where he pleased. We bestow of Our mercy on whom We please and We do not allow to be lost the reward of those who do good". (12:55-56)

Christianity: Joseph Re-United With His Family

The Bible says ": And Joseph made ready his chariot, and went up to meet Israel (Jacob) his father, to Goshen, and presented himself unto him and he fell on his neck and wept on his neck a good while". (Genesis 46:29)

Islam: Joseph Re-United With His Family

The Qur'an states: "Then when they entered the presence of Joseph, he provided a home for his parents with himself and said. "Enter you Egypt (all) in safety if it pleases G'd". (12:99)

Chapter Summary

The importance of the story of Joseph and his brothers cannot be fully expressed by the few verses given in this chapter. However, we hope that we were able to demonstrate that both religions, Christianity and Islam gives similar accounts of this story, and in so doing, stimulated a greater interest in finding the common thread that runs through these two religions.

CHAPTER 7

MOSES AND EGYPT

The story of Moses, as a prophet and a liberator, like the story of Joseph, holds a very significant place in the Bible and the Qur'an. According to the Bible, there was a king who came into power in Egypt who "knew not Joseph." Under his leadership the Hebrews were taken into bondage. G'd eventually raised up Moses to be their liberator.

Both religions, Christianity and Islam give similar accounts of this story. Although it may not surprise many that Ancient Egypt is referenced in the holy scriptures, many may in fact be surprised at how often Moses is mentioned in the Holy Qur'an. As a matter of fact Muhammad The Prophet (pbuh) is referred to as "a man like Moses", in Islamic teachings.

The consistence of the story of Moses in both the Bible and the Qur'an is striking. Note the following verses.

Christianity: Moses Enters Egypt As A Baby

The Bible says: "And when she could no longer hide him (Moses), she took for him an ark of bulrushes and daubed it with slime and with pitch, and put the child therein and she laid it in the flags by the river bank. And his sister stood afar off to see what would be done to him. And the daughter of Pharaoh came down to wash herself at the river: and her maidens walked along by the river's side. And when she saw the ark among the flags, she sent her maid to fetch it.

And when she had opened it she saw the child, and behold the babe wept. And she had compassion on him and said, "this is one of the Hebrews' children." Then said his sister to Pharaoh's daughter, "shall I go and call to thee a nurse of the Hebrew women, that she may nurse the child for you?" And Pharaoh's daughter said to her, "go." And the maid went and called the child's mother. And Pharaoh' daughter said unto her, "take this child away and nurse it for me, and I will give you your wages." And the woman took the child and nursed it.

And the child grew up and she brought him unto Pharaoh's daughter and he became her son. And she called his name Moses, because I drew him out of the water". (Exodus, 2:3-10)

Islam: Moses Enters Egypt As A Baby

The Qur'an states: "And certainly We bestowed on you a favor at another time, when We revealed to your mother what was revealed: Saying put him (Moses) into a basket, then cast it down into the river, then the river shall throw him on the shore; there shall take him up one who is an enemy to Me and an enemy to him. And I cast down upon you love from Me and that you might be brought up before My eyes.

When your sister went and said: " Shall I direct you to one who will take charge of him?" So we brought you back to your mother, that her eye might be cooled and she should not grieve..."(20:37-40)

The Qur'an also states: "These are verses of the Book that makes (things) clear. We rehearse to you some of the story of Moses and Pharaoh in truth, for people who believe. So We sent this inspiration to the mother of Moses: "Suckle (your child), but when you have fears about him, cast him into the river. But fear not nor grieve: For We shall restore him to you and We shall make him one of Our messengers." Then the people of Pharaoh picked him up. He was destined to be an adversary and a cause of sorrow for them. Surely Pharaoh and Haman and their host were men of sin."

The wife of pharaoh said: "a joy of the eye for me and for you. Slay him not. It may be that he will be of use to us or we may adopt him as a son." And-they perceived not (what they were doing). But there came to be a void in the heart of the mother of Moses. She was going to almost disclose his (case) had We not strengthened her heart (with faith), so that she might remain a (firm) believer.

Thus did We restore him to his mother, that her eye might be comforted, that she might not grieve, and that she might know that the promise of G'd is true; but most of them do not understand."(28:2,3,7-13)

Moses Kills a Man

The Bible and the Qur'an relates the incident of Moses' confrontation with an Egyptian in defense of one of his own people. This event was actually a major turning point in his life, because as a result he fled Egypt. While he was out of Egypt he was made a prophet of G'd, and was charged with the responsibility of liberating his people.

Christianity: Moses Killed an Egyptian

The Bible states: "And it came to pass in those days, when Moses was grown, that he went out unto his brethren, and looked on their burdens: and he saw an Egyptian smiting a Hebrew, one of his brethren. And he looked this way and that way and when he saw that there was no man, he slew the Egyptian, and hid him in the sand. And when he went out the second day, behold, two men of the Hebrews fought each other, and he said to him that did wrong, "wherefore smitest thou thy fellow?" And he said (to Moses) "who made thee a prince and a judge over us? intendest thou to kill me, as thou killedst the Egyptian?" And Moses feared and said, " surely this thing is known."

Now when Pharaoh heard this thing, he sought to slay Moses. But Moses fled from the face of Pharaoh, and dwelt in the land of Midian: and he sat down by a well." (Exodus 2:11-15)

Islam: Moses Killed an Egyptian

The Qur'an states: "when Moses reached full age, and was firmly established, We bestowed on him wisdom and knowledge, For surely do We reward those who do good. And he entered the city at a time when its people were not watching; and he found there two men fighting, one of his own religion and the other, of his foes. Now the man of his own religion appealed to him against his foe and Moses struck him with his fist and made an end of him. He (Moses) said: "This is a work of evil, for he (Satan) is an enemy that clearly misleads." He said: "My Lord! Surely I have done harm to myself, so will You forgive me." So He forgave him. Surely He is the Forgiving, the Merciful. He (Moses) said, "My Lord! Because you have bestowed favor on me, I shall never be a backer of the guilty."

"And he was in the city fearing awaiting, when lo! He who had asked his assistance the day before was crying out to him for aid. Musa (Moses) said to him, "You are most surely one clearly in error. So he desired to seize him who was an enemy to them both, he said: "O Moses do you intend to kill me as you killed a person yesterday? You desire nothing but that you should be a tyrant in the land and you do not desire to be of those who act aright." And a man came running from the farthest part of the city. He said, "O Moses surely the chiefs are consulting together to slay you, therefore depart. Surely, I am of those who wish you well. So he (Moses) went forth there from, fearing, awaiting. He said: " My Lord! Deliver me from the unjust people."

And when he (Moses) turned his face towards Madyan he said: Maybe my Lord will guide me in the right path. And when he came to the water of Madyan, he found a group of men watering, and he found besides them two women keeping back (their flock)..." (28:14-23)

Christianity: Moses and the Burning Bush

The Bible informs us that Moses kept the flock of Jethro, his father in law, the priest of Midian: and he led the flock to the backside of the desert, and came to the mountain of G'd, even to Horeb. And the angel of the Lord appeared unto him in a flame of fire out of the midst of a bush: and he looked, and, behold, the bush burned with fire, and the bush was not consumed. And Moses said, " I will now turn aside and see this great sight, why the bush is not burnt." (Exodus 3:1-3).

Islam: Moses and the Burning Bush

The Qur'an informs us that: "When Moses said to his family, surely I see fire, I will bring to you from it some news or I will bring to you therefrom a burning firebrand so that you may warm yourselves. So when he came to it, a voice was heard saying; blessed is whoever is in the fire and whatever is about it. And glory be to G'd, the Lord of the worlds." (27:7-9)

Christianity: Moses Given Signs

The Bible States: "And the Lord said unto him (Moses) what is that in thine hand? And he said, a rod. And he (G'd) said, cast it on the ground, and it became a serpent; and Moses fled from before it. And the Lord said unto Moses, put forth thine hand, and take it by the tail. And he put forth his hand and caught it and it became a rod in his hand.

And the Lord said furthermore unto him. Put now thine hand into thy bosom. And he put his hand into his bosom: And when he took it out, behold, his hand was leprous (white) as snow. And He (G'd) said, put thine hand into thy bosom again. And he put his hand into his bosom again; and plucked it out of his bosom, and, behold it was turned again as his other flesh."(Exodus 4:2-7)

Islam: Moses Given Signs

The Qur'an says that G'd said: "And what is that in your right hand, O Moses?" He said: "It is my rod, on it I beat down fodder for my flocks, and in it I find other uses." He (G'd) said: "Throw it, O Moses!" He threw it and behold! It was a snake active in motion. G'd said: "Seize it and fear not: We shall return it at once to its former condition." (20: 17-21). In another place in the Holy Qur'an it says: "But when he (Moses) saw it moving as if it was a snake, he turned back in retreat, and traced not his steps." (27:10)

"Now put your hand into your bosom and it will come forth white without stain. These are among the nine signs you will take to Pharaoh and his people. For they are a people rebellious in transgression." (27:12)

Christianity: Moses Given His Mission

"And He (G'd) said, draw not nigh hither; put off thy shoes from off thy feet, for the place whereon thou standest is holy ground. Come now therefore, and I will send thee unto Pharaoh that thou mayest bring forth my people the Children of Israel out of Egypt". (Exodus 3:10)

Islam: Moses Given His Mission

"Verily I am your Lord! Therefore (in my Presence) put off your shoes: You are in the sacred valley of Tuwa. I have chosen you. Listen then to the inspiration. Go thou to Pharaoh, for he has indeed transgressed all bounds." (20: 12-13, 24)

Christianity: Moses Asks G'd for Aaron's Help

The Bible says that Moses said unto the Lord, "O my Lord, I am not eloquent, neither heretofore, nor since thou hast spoken unto thy servant; but I am slow of speech, and of slow tongue. And the Lord said unto him, who hath made man's mouth? Or who maketh him the dumb or deaf, or the seeing or the blind? Have not I the Lord? Now therefore go and I will be with thy mouth and teach thee what thou shall say. And he (Moses) said, O my Lord, send, I pray thee, by the hand of him whom thou wilt send. And the anger of the Lord was kindled against Moses, and he (G'd) said, Is not Aaron, the Levite, thy brother? I know that he can speak well. And also behold, he cometh forth to meet thee: And when he seeth thee, he will be glad in his heart. And thou shalt speak unto him and put words in his mouth: And I will be with thy mouth and with his mouth and will teach you what ye shall do. And he (Aaron) shall be thy spokesman unto the people." (Exodus 4:10-16)

Islam: Moses Ask G'd for Aaron's Help

The Qur'an says Moses said: "O my Lord! Expend for me my breast; ease my task for me and remove the impediment from my speech, so they may understand what I say. And give me a minister from my family, Aaron, my brother; add to my strength through him, and make him share my task, that we may celebrate your praise without fault and remember you without fault: For you are He that forever sees us. He (G'd) said: Granted is your prayer, O Moses!" (20:25-36)

Christianity: Moses and Aaron Address Pharaoh

"And afterwards Moses and Aaron went in and told Pharaoh, Thus saith the Lord G'd of Israel, let my people go that they may hold a feast unto me in the wilderness" And Moses was fourscore years old, and Aaron was fourscore and three years old, when they spoke unto Pharaoh. " (Exodus 5:1 and 7:7)

Islam: Moses and Aaron Address Pharaoh

"Moses said, O Pharaoh, I am a messenger from the Lord of the Worlds; One for whom it is right to say nothing but truth about G'd. Now have I come unto you from your Lord with a clear (sign). So let the Children of Israel depart along with me." (7:104, 105)

"We did send Moses aforetime with our signs to Pharaoh and his chiefs: He (Moses) said, I am a messenger of the Lord of the worlds." (43:46)

Christianity: Pharaoh's Response To Moses and Aaron

The Bible states that Pharaoh said, "And Pharaoh said, who is the Lord, that I should obey his voice to let Israel go? I know not the Lord, neither will I let Israel go." (Exodus 5:2)

Islam: Pharaoh's Response To Moses and Aaron

"He (Pharaoh) said: Who then, O Moses; is the Lord of you two?" He (Moses) said, "Our Lord is He who gave to every thing its form and then its guidance." He (Pharaoh) said: "What then is the condition of previous generations?" Moses replied: "The knowledge of that is with my Lord, duly recorded: My Lord never errs nor forgets" (20:49-52)

Then did (Moses) show him the Great Sign, but he (Pharaoh) rejected it and disobeyed, further, he turned his back striving hard. Then he collected (his men) and proclaimed; saying, I am your Lord, Most High" (79:20-24)

Pharaoh said: "O chief! No g'd do I know for you but myself, therefore O Haman! Light me a (kiln to bake bricks) out of clay and build me a lofty palace that I may mount up to the g'd of Moses: But as far as I am concerned, I think (Moses) is a liar.' (28: 38)

The Casting of the Rods

The Bible and the Qur'an relates the event that occurred in the courtyard of Pharaoh's palace in Egypt. Although, there are some variations, concerning, for example, who cast the rod, Moses or Aaron and who cast their rods first, the fact still remains that both scriptures carry this event. With some interpretation and analysis, I am sure we will see that the overall message is the same. Let's see what the Bible and Qur'an says about casting the rods.

Christianity: Casting The Rods

The Bible says, "Moses and Aaron went in unto Pharaoh and they did so as the Lord had commanded: And Aaron cast down his rod before Pharaoh and before his servants and it became a serpent, Then Pharaoh also called the wise men and the sorcerers: Now the magicians of Egypt, they also did in like manner with their enchantments. For, every man cast down his rod. And they became serpents, but Aaron's rod swallowed up their rods." (Exodus: 7:10-12)

Islam: Casting The Rods

According the Qur'an Pharaoh said, "his (Moses') plan is to get you out of your land: Then what is it you counsel? Pharaoh asked his advisors. They said, keep him (Moses) and his brother in suspense (for a while) and send to the cities men to collect and bring up to thee all sorcerers well-versed." (7:110-112)

"So the sorcerers were got together for the appointment of a day well-known. The people were told: Are you (now) assembled? That we may follow the sorcerers if they win? So when the sorcerers arrived, they said to Pharaoh. "Of course, shall we have a (suitable) reward if we win?" He said: "Yes (and more) for you shall in that case be (raised to posts) nearest (to my person)." Moses said to them: Throw you that which you are about to throw. So they threw their rods, and said: "By the might of Pharaoh, it is we who will certainly win!" Then Moses threw his rod, when behold it straightway swallowed up all the falsehoods, which they faked!   Then did the sorcerers fall down prostate in adoration, saying: "We believe in the Lord of the worlds. The Lord of Moses and Aaron." (26:38-48)

In another place in the Qur'an it says that the sorcerers said: "O Moses! Will you throw (first) or shall we have the (first) throw?" And Moses said, "You throw (first)." So when they threw, they bewitched the eyes of the people, and struck fear into them; for they showed a great magic. We put it into Moses' mind by inspiration: "Throw (now) your rod:" and behold! It swallowed up straightway all the falsehoods which they faked!" (7:115-117)

Christianity: Moses Leads His People Out of Egypt

The Bible says,"Pharaoh called for Moses and Aaron by night and said, rise up and get you forth from among my people, both you and the Children of Israel, and go serve the Lord, as you have said. Also take your flocks and your herds, as you have said and be gone; and bless me also."
(Exodus 12: 31-32)

Islam: Moses Leads His People Out of Egypt

The Qur'an says that by inspiration "We told Moses, travel by night with My servants, for surely you shall be pursued. Then Pharaoh sent heralds to (all) the cities, saying, "These (Israelites) are but a small band and they are raging furiously against us, but we are a multitude amply fore-warned." So We expelled them (The Egyptians) from gardens, springs, treasures and every kind of honorable position. Thus it was, but We made the Children of Israel inheritors of such things."(26: 53-60)

Christianity: The Parting of the Red Sea

"And Moses streched out his hand over the sea: and the Lord caused the sea to go back by a strong east wind all that night and made the sea dry land and the waters were divided. And the Children of Israel went into the midst of the sea upon dry ground: and the waters were a wall unto them on their right hand and on their left.

And the Egyptians pursued and went in after them to the midst of the sea, even all Pharaoh's horses, his chariots and his horsemen. And the Lord said unto Moses, stretch out thine hand over the sea that the waters may come again upon the Egyptians, upon their chariots and upon their horsemen" (Exodus 14:21-26)

Islam: The Parting of the Red Sea

The Qur'an says: "Then we told Moses by inspiration: Strike the sea with your rod. So it divided and each separate part became like the huge firm mass of a mountain. And We made the other party (the Egyptians) approach there. We delivered Moses and all who were with him, But We drowned the others. Verily in this is a sign: But most of them do not believe. And verily your Lord is He, the Exalted in might, Most Merciful". (26: 64-69)

Christianity: Moses Receives Revelation From G'd

"And the Lord said unto Moses, come up to me into the mount, and be there; and I will give you tablets of stone and a law and commandments which I have written; that thou mayest teach them". (Exodus 24:12)

Islam: Moses Receives Revelation From G'd

"We did reveal to Moses the Book after We had destroyed the earlier generations (to give) insight to men and guidance and mercy that they might receive admonition". (28:43)

The Qur'an also states: "And We ordained laws for him in the Tablets in all matters, both commanding and explaining all things (and said): Take and hold these with firmness, and enjoin your people to hold fast by the best in the precepts". (7:145)

Chapter Summary

Moses was a true liberator. The Ancient Egyptians were very wise. They had mastered the physical sciences and were well versed in mental and spiritual logic. The Bible and the Qur'an clearly shows similar accounts of the huge job that Moses had to do. Both religions show that G'd was with Moses from the time he was born until the time he died. G'd had written the script for his life, just as He has written for ours. This chapter, as did the others, gives us strong proof that the essence of the Bible and the Qur'an are from the same source.

CHAPTER 8

ZECHARIAHS AND JOHN

Christianity and Islam explain the birth of John and his mission as a fore-runner to Jesus. The Bible and the Qur'an give a similar account of Zechariahs and his wife's reaction when they were told that they were going to have a son. Let us consider the following verses.

Christianity: Zechariahs' Prayer is Answered

According to the Holy Bible: "There was in the Days of Herod, the king of Judea, a certain priest, named Zechariahs of the course of Abia, and his wife was of the daughters of Aaron and her name was Elisabeth. And they were both righteous before G'd, walking in all the commandments and ordinances of the Lord, blameless. And they had no child, because that Elisabeth was barren, and they both were now well stricken in years.

And their appeared unto Zechariahs an angel of the Lord standing on the right side of the altar of incense. The angel said unto him, fear not for your prayer is heard; and your wife Elisabeth shall bear you a son and you shalt call his name John". For he shall be great in the sight of the Lord.

And Zechariahs said unto the angel, whereby shall I know this, for I am an old man, and my wife well stricken in years. And the angel answering said unto him, I am Gabriel, that stand in the presence of G'd, and am sent to speak unto you and to show you these glad tidings. And behold thou shall be dumb and not able to speak until the day that these things shall be performed" (Luke, 1: 5-7,11,13,15,18-20)

Islam: Zechariahs' Prayer is Answered

According to the Qur'an: "Zechariahs prayed unto his Lord and said: My Lord! Bestow upon me of Your bounty goodly offspring. For You are the Hearer of prayers. And the angel called to him as he stood praying in the prayer place. G'd giveth you glad tidings of John (Yayah) to confirm a word from G'd, chaste, a prophet of the righteous. He said: My Lord! How can I have a son when age has overtaken me already and my wife is barren? He said: G'd does what He wills. He (Zechariahs) said: My Lord appoint a token for me. It was said: The token unto you (shall be) that you shall not speak unto mankind three days except by sign. Remember your Lord much, and praise (Him) in the early hours of the night and morning." (3: 38-41)

The Qur'an also says: "A reminder of the mercy of Your Lord unto His servant Zechariah. (It was said unto him) O Zechariah: Lo! We bring you tidings of a son whose name is John; We have given the same name to none before him.

He said: My Lord! How can I have a son when my wife is barren and I have reached infirm old age?

He (G'd) said: So (it will be) your Lord saith it is easy for Me, even as I created you before when you was non-existent." (19: 2-11)

Chapter Summary

The information presented in this chapter about the birth of John suggests that his birth was somewhat of a miracle. It is interesting to note that this occurred shortly before the miraculous birth of Jesus. It seems that both scriptures are telling us that Almighty G'd is in charge at all times.

CHAPTER 9

MARY AND JESUS

It is extremely important that the reader clearly understands that both of these religions hold Jesus in the highest esteem. The Bible and the Qur'an gives almost identical accounts of his birth. His mother Mary is presented in Islam as a woman of honor. In fact an entire chapter of the Qur'an is named after her. It is also reported that Prophet Muhammad (pbuh) said that at the end of time he and Christ Jesus would be together.

Christianity: Angel Visits Mary to Inform Her of the Birth of Jesus

According to the Bible: "The angel came unto her (Mary) and said, Hail, you that are highly favored, the Lord is with you. Blessed are you among women. Behold you shall conceive in your womb and bring forth a son, and shall call his name Jesus. Then said Mary unto the angel how shall this be, seeing I know not a man? And the angel answered and said unto her, The Holy Ghost shall come upon you and the power of the Highest shall overshadow you." (Luke 1: 28,31,34,35)

Islam: Angel Visits Mary to Inform Her of the Birth of Jesus

The Qur'an says: "Behold! The angels said: "O Mary! G'd giveth thee glad tidings of a word from Him: his name will be Christ Jesus, the son of Mary, held in honor in this world and the Hereafter and of (the company of) those Nearest to God; "He shall speak to the people in childhood and in maturity. And he shall be of the righteous. "She said: "O my Lord! How shall I have a son when no man hath touched me? He said: Even so G'd created what He willeth:

When He hath decreed a plan, He but saith to it, `be and it is! "And G'd will teach him The Book and Wisdom, The Law and The Gospel" (3: 45-48)

Christianity: Concerning Christ Jesus

According to the Bible Jesus performed miracles, preached love, defended the oppressed and educated those who would listen. Listed below are some of his teachings according to the Bible:

➢ Blessed are the peacemakers for they shall be called the children of G'd,

➢ Blessed are the humble in spirit for theirs is the kingdom of heaven.

➢ Blessed are the meek: for they shall inherit the earth:

➢ Blessed are they which do hunger and thirst after righteousness: for they shall be filled.

➢ Blessed are the merciful: for they shall obtain mercy.

➢ Blessed are the pure in heart: for they shall see G'd,

➢ Blessed are they which are persecuted for righteousness' sake: for theirs is the kingdom of heaven, (Matthew 5:3 -10)

➢ "And when thou prayest, thou shalt not be as the hypocrites are: for they love to pray standing in the synagogues and in the corners of the streets, that they may be seen of men. Verily I say unto you, they have their reward;"(Matthew 6:5)

➢ No man can serve two masters: for either he will hate the one, and love the other; or else he will hold to the one, and despise the other. Ye cannot serve G'd and mammon.

> But seek ye first the kingdom of G'd, and his righteousness; and all these things shall be added unto you.

> Ask and it shall be given you; seek and ye shall find; knock and it shall be opened unto you.

> Even so every good tree bringeth forth good fruit; but a corrupt tree bringeth forth evil fruit.

> And fear not them which kill the body, but are not able to kill the soul: but rather fear him which is able to destroy both soul and body in hell.

> Behold I send you forth as sheep in the midst of wolves: be ye therefore wise as serpents, and harmless as doves". (Matthew 10: 16)

The Names of the Twelve Disciples

According to the Bible the twelve disciples were:

1. Simon, who is called Peter
2. Andrew
3. James the son of Zebedee
4. John
5. Philip
6. Bartholomew
7. Thomas
8. Matthew
9. James the son of Alphae'us and Lebbae'us
10. Thaddae'us
11. Simon, the Canaanite
12. Judas Iscariot

Islam: Concerning Christ Jesus

When Jesus found unbelief on their part he said: `` Who will be my helpers to (the work of) G'd? `` Said the Disciples: "We are G'd's helpers: We believe in God, and do thou bear witness that we are those who submit to G'd". (3: 52)

"Behold! The Disciples said: O Jesus the son of Mary! Can thy Lord send down to us a table set (with viands) from heaven?"Said Jesus: "Fear G'd, if ye have faith" They said: "We only wish to eat thereof and satisfy our hearts, and to know that thou hast indeed told us the truth; and that we ourselves may be witnesses to the miracle."

Said Jesus son of Mary: "O G'd our Lord! Send us from heaven a Table set, that there may be for us –for the first and the last of us-a solemn festival and a sign from you, and provide for our sustenance for Thou art the best of Sustainer"(**5**: 115,118)

The Qur'an says; "And we made the son of Mary and his mother as a sign: We gave them both Shelter on high ground, affording rest and security and furnished with springs."(23:50)

"The similitude of Jesus before God is as that of Adam; He created him from dust, Then said to him: "Be and he was" (3: 59)

" . . . We ordained in the hearts of those who follow him (Jesus) compassion and mercy." (57: 27)

"And in their footsteps We sent Jesus the son of Mary, confirming The Law that had come before him: We sent him the Gospel: Therein was guidance and light, and confirmation of the Law that had come before him: A guidance and an admonition to those who fear G'd." (5: 49)

Chapter Summary

This chapter highlights the fact that Jesus is held in great honor in Islam as well as in Christianity. It clearly shows that Muslims believe in the "immaculate conception" also. G'd reminds us in the Qur'an that the birth of Jesus is like that of Adam. He created him from dust. G'd made Adam without the help of a man or woman.

CHAPTER 10

CONNECTING THE KNOWLEDGE

The Bible and The Qur'an contains volumes of knowledge for the benefit of humanity. As I have already pointed out in previous chapters, the similarities between Christianity and Islam is vast. In this last chapter I hope to show some of the similarities that are alluded to, implied or inferred. The Bible says that King Solomon, a prophet of G'd said: "Get knowledge, get wisdom, but with all thy getting, get an understanding." This suggests that what stands-under the surface, sometimes, may be more enlightening than that which is above the surface. In the Bible, Jesus used some very interesting and enlightening parabales when addressing his disciple's. In some cases those parables carried some messages that were more powerful and more rich in meaning than his plain talk. Sometimes when knowledge is connected, a greater appreciation is given to it.

In keeping with the objective of this work, let us now turn our attention to the importance of Solomon's Temple.

Solomon's Temple

The Bible and the Qur'an says that Solomon was blessed with a wealth of knowledge and wisdom. In the Bible it informs us that G'd said to Solomon: "Behold, I have done according to thy words: lo, I have given thee a wise and an understanding heart." (1Kings 3:12) The Qur'an states: "We gave knowledge to David and Solomon; and they both said 'All praises be to G'd, Who has favored us above many of his servants who believe."(27: 15)

The story of Solomon stands out in the Qur'an for several reasons, but one of the most important reasons is that one of the chapters that gives information about Solomon, contains the expression "With the Name of G'd the Most Gracious, Most Merciful", twice. It should be noted that there are **114 chapters** in the Qur'an. All except one chapter begins with the words **"With the Name of G'd the Most Gracious, the Most Merciful.** However, this expression still occurs 114 times in the Qur'an because **it is repeated twice in chapter 27. It appears in the beginning of that chapter and it also appears in verse 30 of that same chapter. It appears in Solomon's letter to the Queen of Sheba.** The only chapter in the Qur'an that does not begin with the expression, With The Name of G'd the Most Gracious, The Most Merciful is chapter nine.

It is reported that Solomon, while having the temple built for the glorification of G'd, acknowledged, "This temple and the heavens of heavens cannot contain You." (IIChronicles 6:18) The Bible in describing Solomon's Temple gives detailed information about how many workers were involved; the measurements, the decorations etc. The Bible also makes mention of a Temple that was built without hands or the knocking of hammers. (1Kings 6:7) It reports that Jesus said "The kingdom of G'd is within." Jesus also referred to himself as a temple. According to the Bible Jesus said, "Destroy this temple, and in three days I will raise it up." (John 2:19) This suggests that the greater concern should be on the spiritual temple, the inner person, the soul. The Bible tells us that in entering Solomon's Temple a person had to go pass two pillars, one on the right called Jachin and one on the left, called Boaz. (1Kings 7:15-22 and IIChronicles 3:15, 4:12,13). According to some reports the stairs leading up to the entrance consisted of a set of three, five and seven steps.

The Spiritual Temple

The Bible says that Jesus said "As a man thinketh in his heart, so is he. It is reported that Muhammad, the Prophet (pbuh) said that there is a morsel of flesh in the body, and that if it is good the whole body is good and if it is bad then the whole body is bad. When he was asked what is it, he said, "It is the heart." Our true self is the inner being. The Bible and the Qur'an both says that the human being is not alive until his soul becomes alive. In Genesis it says that G'd breathed into Adam's nostrils and then he became a living soul. The Qur'an says that G'd said to the angels that they did not have to submit to Adam until "I have breathed into him something of My spirit"(15: 26-29)

If we can consider, the possibility, that Solomon's Temple, in some way symbolizes the human being and his beautiful and marvelous attributes, inner qualities and potential, then the idea that G'd is communicating a higher message to us, in the story of the building of Solomon's Temple, should be much more acceptable. The greater message is, what went into the making of a human being; the spiritual temple. As I have already quoted from the Bible there were two pillars at the entrance of Solomon's Temple. What do they represent in the human being? They represent the conscious and the sub-conscious. Our mind takes in information on a conscious and a sub-conscious level. Those pillars may also symbolize our two ears or two eyes that are located close to the temple on either side of our forehead.

The Importance of Three, Five and Seven in Religion:

We as human beings are often seen as a physical, mental and sprital creation, having material rational and sprital or religious concerns. According to religion, G'd created us as a physical, mental and sprital being, therefore when He addresses us, He does so on one or more of these levels. The Bible says that there were *three* in the Garden of Eden; Adam, Eve and the Serpent and all *three* of them were cast out of the garden. The Qur'an says that G'd said to

Adam, his wife and Satan, "get you down from here…" The Qur'an also gives a picture of *three* beings when G'd addressed the angels and said, "I am making a ruler in the earth". It says that G'd told the angels to submit to Adam and they all did except Iblis, who was a jinn. This clearly shows that there were *three*, the human being, the angels and the jinn.

In the Holy Scriptures the *three* levels or aspects of the human being are classified and symbolized under various names, titles and events. For example the Bible says that Noah had three sons name Sham, Ham and Japheth. The Qur'an informs us of *three* levels or types of soul, called, amaara (commanding) la'wwaama (self accusing) and mutma'ina (peaceful, tranquil). The Bible says, "G'd breathed into his nostrils the breath of life and he became a living soul." It also says, "what would it profit a man to gain the whole world but lose his soul?" The Qur'an says that G'd has given balance and proportion to the soul. It also says that G'd enlightened the soul in such a way that it naturally seeks the light of truth and is regardful of G'd. It further explains that the person who invests in their soul will be successful, and whoever neglects their soul will fail. (91:7-10)

In a chapter in the Qur'an, entitled The Bee, G'd mentions *three* levels or functions of the mind. After drawing our attention to His vast creation with its beautiful colors, symmetry, the flowing of water, the growth of trees, vegetation, and the movement of the sun, moon and stars and their benefit to us, He says there are signs in these things for those who **reflect** (yatafakkaruun), those who **reason,** (ya'qiluun) and those who **think** with a focus (yadhakkaruun). (16: 11-13)

When we read the scriptures, keeping in focus the fact that the sacred scriptures themselves, informs us that our true self is the inner self, and that it has *three* levels of the soul, three aspects of the mind, as well as our physical, mental and spiritual developments, then whenever we see a reference to three in the scriptures, perhaps we should consider the possibility that it is alluding to those *three* levels in the human being. For example, the Bible says that there was a man name Baalam who wanted to travel somewhere that G'd didn't want him to go. He got on a donkey to ride; but the donkey wouldn't move, so Baalam struck the donkey *three* times. The Bible says that the donkey turned his head around and looked at Baalam and asked him "why have you struck me these *three* times."(Numbers 22: 22-32) According to some symbolic teachings, the donkey represents the working masses of people. In America, the symbol of the Democratic Party is a donkey. Perhaps Baalam was trying to take the soul or mind of the people somewhere that G'd didn't want them to go. The story goes on to say that the reason the donkey did not move is because he saw an angel with a flaming sword standing in front of him, that Balaam did not see. Sometimes G'd will reveal something to the common people before He reveal it to the leaders. In fact the overwhelming number of prophets and messengers that have been raised up by G'd were from the common people.

In the religion of Islam it is reported that Muhammad the Prophet (pbuh) was from the common people. He use to go to the cave Hira in Arabia where he would reflect, reason and think over the condition of his people and the world. One night the angel Gabriel appeared unto him and gripped and squeezed his soul and mind *three* times, commanding him to "read!" each time. The first two times Muhammad replied, "I cannot read." But, the *third* time he began to read. That was the beginning of the Revelation of the Qur'an and the beginning of his life as a prophet and messenger of G'd. He was raised up from Muhammad to Prophet Muhammad (pbuh). This is an important connection because the Bible says that Jesus rose on the *third* day and that when he was younger he was missing for three days and when his parents found him he was in the temple "sitting in the midst of the doctors, both hearing them and asking them questions."(Luke 2:46-50) We also read in the Bible that there was a little book that was taken to *three* men, who were asked to "read" it. The first two could not read it but the third man read it. (Isaiah 29: 11, 12,18 and Revelation 5:1-4)

In the book of Kings, it is written that Elijah raised the widow's son from the dead by pressing him three times. "And he stretched himself upon the child *three* times, and cried unto the Lord and said, O Lord my G'd, I pray thee, let this child's soul come into him again. And the Lord heard the voice of Elijah; and the soul of the child came into him again, and he was revived."(17:21-24) Let us keep in mind what has already been said about the levels of the soul. The Bible and the Qur'an informs us that Joseph, in his vision saw *three* lights bowing to him; the sun, moon and stars.

In concluding our discussion on the significance of three in religion it should be noted that the Bible says that the king of Babylon, Nebuchadnezzar, put *three* boys named Sha-drach, Me-shach and Abed-nego into the fiery furnace for refusing to worship the false g'ds of Babylon. It says that the king told the furnace keeper to make the fire seven times hotter. When the king came back to see their ashes, he was surprise because they were not burned. In fact, it says he thought he saw a fourth person in the furnace. Perhaps this represents the innate ability of the *three* levels of the soul to endure the heat of oppression because of G'd's ever-present mercy.

It is interesting to note that the *three* religions, Judaism, Christianity and Islam are united in Abraham, who according to the Qur'an, while searching for the proper concept of G'd at night, looked at three lights in the sky. The Qur'an says that when the night covered him over he looked at a star and said, "this is my lord; but when it set, he said, "I love not that which sets." Then when he saw the moon rising he said, " This is my lord." When it set he said: "If my

Lord does not guide me, I will be of those who go astray." Then he saw the sun rising and he said: "This is my Lord, this is the greatest! When it set he said: "O my people I am free from false worship. For me, I have set my face firmly and truly towards Him Who created the heavens and the earth, and never shall I give partners to G'd."(6: 76-79)

I mention this story about Abraham because the Bible says that Jesus is traced back to Abraham. In the first chapter and verse of Matthew, it reads, "The book of the generation of Jesus Christ, the son of David, the son of Abraham." In the religion of Islam it is understood that Prophet Muhammad is traced back to Abraham through Ishmael. The Qur'an states clearly that the order or way of Prophet Muhammad is after that of Abraham. (16:123) As G'd showed respect for each level of Abraham's soul and mind by showing him *three* lights as a way of bringing him to the Ultimate Truth, He did the same for Abraham's descendents, when according to Christianity and the Bible he rose on the third day. This is also seen in the fact that Islam teaches that God's angel, Gabriel, gripped or squeezed Muhammad three times. G'd created the levels of the soul and mind in us and He shows respect for each level when He addresses us. Especially when He is bringing us to the light.

Concerning the *three* boys that were put in the fiery furnace, I understand them to also represent the three Abrahamic Religions. The Bible says that those three boys were skilled and were making contributions to the world, and were true in faith. The followers of the three Abrahamic religions, like those *three* boys, have made major contributions to the world. Similarly, at some point in history, each of them was cast into the fiery furnace as well. They all have experienced the fire of oppression hatred and bigotry. But the true in faith always survived because of G'd's mercy and protection. In the Qur'an G'd says the Believers are victorious, the winners. Those who oppose G'd and religion has never been able to destroy the human beings belief in G'd, even when they make the fire seven times hotter. There will always be true and faithful believers in G'd. (23: 1)

Concerning Solomon and the temple, it should be clear that it also alludes to the spiritual temple within. The word Solomon means peace. It comes from the same root or word as the words Islam and Muslim come from. As we mentioned in the introduction these words come from the Arabic word "salama." The root is SLM, three letters. In Arabic Solomon is spelled Sulaimaan. He was the third king of Jerusalem. This suggests that he symbolizes the *third* level of the soul, because, according to the Qur'an, that soul is the soul at peace, tranquil. Therefore we can understand Solomon's Temple to be "The Temple of peace" in which you have to go pass two pillars in order to enter. Now let us discuss the importance of five in religion.

The Significance of Five in Religion

We as human beings have *five* senses; sight, hearing, touch, taste and smell. These senses are essential for the growth and development of our minds. It is through the five senses that we receive information from the outer world, the environment. If all the *five* senses were missing we would only have the outer shell or flesh body of a human being, not the true life and identity of a human being.

In creating the human pattern and structure, G'd made *five* outstanding in our life, For example, each of our hands have *five* fingers. Our hands are very important. We need them to work, build, write etc. We also have five toes on each foot. Our feet serve as the foundation upon which we stand. They allow us to walk and move about in the world.

Since G'd created us and made *five* outstanding and important in our life, it seems logical that He would also address *five* when communicating to us in His divine revelations. The first Books of the Bible are called "The *Five* Books of Moses", which are:

1. Genesis

2. Exodus

3. Leviticus

4. Numbers

5. Deuteronomy

It should not surprise us then, that the east entrance to the Holy Place, the Sanctuary, inside the Tabernacle that was erected by Moses, in the desert, was supported be *five* pillars, which were spaced *five* cubits apart. (Exodus 36:38). It is also reported that inside the sanctuary in Solomon's Temple there were *five* tables on the right side and *five* on the left, and *five* candles on the right and *five* on the left. (II Chronicles 4:7-8). It can be reasoned that these five are referring to the *five* in the human temple. As we have already pointed out the five toes are apart of our foundation, our feet. Tables serve as supports, as a foundation. Candles stand perpendicular; *five* on the right and *five* on the left symbolizes the *five* fingers on our right and left hands. If we hold our hands up with our fingers extended a little, they would resemble candles. G'd's message is profound, He is letting us know that Solomon's Temple was to be a symbol of the human being and society and that our *five* senses are to serve as lights and supports for our inner life.

Continuing with our discussion on the significance of the *five* let us look briefly at the story of David and Goliath.

David, Goliath and Five Smooth Stones:

The Bible and the Qur'an both mention David and Goliath, however, the Bible gives greater details. The Qur'an states: "When they advanced to meet Goliath and his forces, they prayed: Our Lord! Pour out patience on us and make our steps firm: Help us against those that reject faith. By G'd's Will they routed them, and David slew Goliath. And G'd gave him (David) power and wisdom and taught him whatever He willed. And did not G'd check one set of people by means of another, the earth would indeed be full of mischief: But G'd is full of bounty to all the worlds."
(2: 250, 251)

According to the Bible David was a natural human being. He had *five* senses, *five* fingers on each hand and *five* toes on each foot, two eyes, etc. He decided to do battle with an unnatural giant, who had six fingers on each hand and six toes on each foot and one eye in the center of his forehead. When he and David met for battle, it is reported that David reached into the water and took out five smooth stones and put one in his slang –shot and hit Goliath in his head and knocked him down on the ground. He then took Goliath's sword and cut his head off. (I Samuel 17: 40, 49-51, II Samuel 21:20 and I Chronicle 20:6)

It is interesting to note that David took the *five* stones from the water. Science and religion tells us that all life comes from water. Before we are born from our mother's we live in her body enclosed in water. Once her "water breaks", that is a sign that it is almost time for the baby to be born. David reaching into the water indicates that he reached into his original innocent nature, the baby nature and pulled out his five common senses. Our senses begin to develop in the water, in our mothers. The earth is called mother earth. We come from the water that is on the earth. G'd is letting us know that David was able to defeat Goliath with common sense and natural intelligence. By concentrating, David was able to bring his *five* senses together as one, serving one purpose, the defeat of Goliath.

Continuing further with our discussion on the importance of *five* in religion, we find that the Bible says that Jesus was the son of David (Matthew Chapter 1 verse 1). Jesus, like David used *five* also. It is reported that Jesus fed the multitude of people with two fish and *five* loaves of bread. Bread adds weight to the physical body, therefore, the *five* loaves of bread represents the five senses that dominate the physical body, called the sensory body. Jesus was teaching the people how they should clean and take care of themselves. He was giving them a basic common sense message. He was also educating them rationally and spiritually. The two fish represent a different kind of message than the bread. Fish live in the water and they are called brain food. Groupings of fish are called schools. Fish swim fast in water just as our thoughts move swiftly in our minds fish represents moral thoughts and ideas. The Bible and Qur'an say that a big fish swallowed Jonah. It simply means he was consumed by his own idea of what message should have been preached to the city Nineveh. When he realized that he wasn't thinking right he prayed to G'd for forgiveness and mercy. G'd forgave him and delivered him from that kind of thinking.

After Jesus came Muhammad, a natural man with *five* senses, *five* fingers on each hand and *five* toes on each foot like all other human beings. In the Qur'an it says that G'd told Muhammad The Prophet to tell the people that he (Muhammad) is a mortal human being, just like them. The first revelation from G'd to Muhammad consisted of *five* verses. One night while he was in the cave Hira, thinking and reflecting, the angel Gabriel gave him *five* verses from the Qur'an, which transformed him from Muhammad to Prophet Muhammad. Those verses read as follows:

1. Read! With the name of your Lord Who created you;

2. Created mankind from a clot

3. Read! And your Lord is Most Generous

4. He Who taught (the use of) the pen,

5. Taught mankind what it did not know before (96: 1-5)

The night that this occurred is called "The Night of Power". When G'd describe that night in the Qur'an He does so in five verses, as follows:

1. We have indeed sent this down in the Night of Power

2. And what will explain to you what the Night of Power is?

3. The Night of Power is better than a thousand months.

4. Therein come down the angels and the Spirit by G'd's permission on every affair

5. Peace! Until the rise of dawn. (97: 1-5)

The Religion of Islam is structured upon *five*. The *five* pillars are:

1. Witness that there is only one G'd

2. Salat (Prayer)

3. Zakat (Charity)

4. Saum Fasting during the month of Ramadan

5. Hajj (Pilgrimage to Makkah)

It is reported that Prophet Muhammad was asked, "What is Islam?" He replied: "Islam is built upon *five*." It is also reported that Prophet Muhammad said: "Take charge of *five* before *five* takes charge of you." In Islam Muslims are obligated to make at least five mandatory prayers.

1. Dawn Prayer

2. Noon Prayer

3. Afternoon Prayer

4. Sunset Prayer

5. Evening Prayer

The religion of Islam is dominated by *five* just as the human being is because, Islam is designed to address the human being. In fact the Qur'an states clearly that Islam is patterned after the excellent nature in which G'd created the human being. (30:30)

Now that we have shown the significance of five in religion, let us turn our attention to the importance of seven.

The Importance of Seven in Religion

In religion *seven* is a mystical number that has come to represent completion. In Genesis it says that on the *seventh* day G'd rested. He brought the creation to its completion .He rested the creation, meaning it was set, fixed, done. As the Bible says "It is done." Keep in mind that we are looking at *seven* in relations to Solomon's Temple as a symbol of the human/spiritual temple. As I have already mentioned, that according to some reports the staircase leading up into Solomon's Temple consisted of a set of three, five and *seven* steps which represent certain aspects of the human being. I have also pointed out that G'd address these aspects in scripture.

The Qur'an identifies the seven stages of human development in a chapter entitled, " The Believers". It says:

1. And certainly We created man of an extract of clay.

2. Then We made him a small seed in a firm resting place.

3. Then We made the seed a clot.

4. Then we made the clot a lump of chewed flesh,

5. Then We made (in) the lump of chewed flesh bones.

6. Then We clothed the bones with skin.

7. Then We caused it to grow into another creation, the inner life. (23: 14,15)

Each of these stages symbolizes something very important in the human being. Although each stage is described in terms that denote physical development, they actually refer to our spiritual life and development. G'd gives us a clue, by stating in that same chapter; "And certainly We made above you *seven* tracks..."(23: 16) In Islam it is reported that Prophet Muhammad (pbuh) had a vision in which he was taken by the angel Gabriel from Mecca to Jerusalem. From there he was taken up to *seven* heavens. On each level he met one of the previous prophets.

1. Adam

2. Jesus and John

3. Joseph

4. Idris (Enoch)

5. Aaron

6. Moses

7. Abraham

It is said that Muhammad greeted each of them in peace and they greeted him in peace. Although each of the prophets was a real human being, in this report they represent a stage in human development.

Adam symbolizes the human entity, the human potential. From the human potential come the achievements.

Jesus symbolizes the spirit and John symbolizes the water, morality, because he was responsible for baptizing the people.

Joseph alludes to the intuitive aspect of the mind, because he had the ability to interpret dreams. He had insight.

Idris (Enoch) represents that ability in the human being to record and preserve knowledge and ideas for the culture. He was a scribe.

Aaron symbolizes the potential in the human being to express ourselves with clear speech. He represents language.

Moses is a sign of laws, rules, and the human structure. He also represents the freedom urge, the unyielding spirit in us to overcome all forms of oppression.

Abraham represents our commitment to faith in G'd and our desire for rational understanding, He also symbolizes universal vision, meaning that we have it in us naturally to see all human beings as one human family. That is why he is called the "Father of all the nations and the Friend of G'd."

Muhammad was shown all of these stages in him that also exist in all of us and he greeted them in peace. The expression of peace that was given between Muhammad and the other prophets is intended to inform that our development is not in conflict, but in agreement. It is a natural, peaceful development. These *seven* stages of development have been pondered over since ancient times.

For thousands of years man has been seeking to know himself. The study of ancient Egypt, Greece and other ancient civilizations reveal that they were fascinated with the mystery of human life. The wise men of Ancient Egypt developed entire schools, called Mystery Systems devoted to the physical, mental and spiritual study of the human being.

The great quest was for man to "know yourself." The ancient wise, considered the knowledge of human development as sacred. That knowledge was seen as being completely sealed. In Ancient Egypt they had a myth of a woman called Isis. It was said that she wore *seven* veils. The moon, because of its *seven* phases that are visible to the eye, symbolized her.

The Bible informs us of a book that had *seven* seals, meaning that it was completely locked up. *Seven* represents completion. The Bible tells us that there was a man who wanted the knowledge so bad that he wept and cried because he could not find anyone who could break the *seven* seals and reveal the knowledge of the *seven* stages of human development.

In the Book of Revelations it says: "And I saw in the right hand of him that sat on the throne a book written within and on the backside, sealed with *seven* seals. And I saw a strong angel proclaiming with a loud voice, "who is worthy to open the book, and to loose the *seven* seals thereof?" And no man in heaven, nor in earth, neither under the earth, was able to open the book, neither to look thereon. And I wept much, because no man was found worthy to open and to read the book, neither to look thereon. (Bible: Revelation 5:1-4) In Isaiah there is also mentioned a book that is sealed.

The book of *seven* seals can be understood as symbolizing the *seven* stages in the human being. The Bible does tell us of a man whose strength was in his *seven* locks of hair it was a secret until he revealed the secret to a woman named Delilah. His name was Sampson. (Judges 16: 13, 19) The Bible also tells us of another man who was referred to as *seven,* by his mother when he was born. Her name was Hannah, she was barren, because as the Bible says, "because G' d had shut up her womb." She eventually had a child. His name was Samuel (I Samuel 1: 6, and 2: 5) This clearly shows us that *seven* is connected to the human being in the scriptures. The scriptures also tell us that Hagar ran to and fro *seven* times searching for water for her baby. In commemoration of Hagar's search, during hajj, pilgrimage to Mecca, Muslims must go between two hills *seven* times. They must also circle the Kabah *seven* times. The first chapter of the Qur'an is called Al-Fatiha, which means the opening. It consists of *seven* verses. It represents the essence of the Qur'an. Each of the *seven* verses can be seen as an expression from the *seven* levels in the human being.

Chapter Summary

In concluding this chapter, I hope I was able to share some information that shows the similarities between Christianity and Islam. The inner value in all of us cannot be fully measured. The spiritual temple was given to us by G'd and we must take care of it and respect it just as we respect our physical houses of worship. G'd made a marvelous creation when He made the human being. He was merciful to us when he decided to send his divine revelations at various points in the span of human existence and by raising up enlightened men and women to help us along the way. These two religions are much closer than most of us realize.

Conclusion

The purpose of this work is to show the similarities in the teachings of Christianity and Islam using both of their Holy Books. I also wanted to show that actually the Qur'an and the Bible are not necessarily two completely separate books but are in fact a continuation of one divine revelation from G'd.

After reading a lecture by Imam Warith Deen Mohammed, leader of the Muslim American Society, in the Muslim Journal, wherein he explained, that the entire Qur'an given to Muhammed The Prophet is actually another reading of the previous scriptures. He indicated that the Bible and

Qur'an are not separate. He also pointed out that Muhammed The Prophet is not to be seen as separate from all the other prophets.

Because of my great respect for him and my appreciation for the great work that he is doing, I approached this work keeping in mind what I read that he said, as well. Our hope is that as a result of this book there can be greater understanding and respect for each other's Faith. I tried to cover the major aspects of both religions; belief in G'd prayer, fasting, belief in angels and the Day of judgment, to name a few. I felt it was important to share some information with the reader about some of the prophets that are mentioned in the Bible and the Qur'an in hopes of showing the compatibility. The similarities in the teachings of Christianity and Islam are so vast, volumes can be written. In closing, let me leave you with the following words.

The world is a different place now than it was before September 11, 2001. It appears to me that this is the time for humanity to try harder to find the " road to peace". What do you think?

Suggested Readings

Holy Qur'an

Holy Bible

The Champion We Have In Common: The Dynamic African American Soul-Part I,Imam W. Deen Mohammed, W.D.M. Ministry Publications, Hazel Crest, IL, 2001

AL-Islam, Unity and Leadership, Imam W. Deen Mohammed The Sense Maker, Chicago, IL 1991

The Bible The Quran and Science, Maurice, Bucaille, Sighers Publishers, Paris France 1982

Abraham's Legacy: Ancient Wisdom and Modern Reality, Mustafa EL-Amin, New Mind Productions, Jersey City, NJ, 1988

Freemasonry Ancient Egypt and The Islamic Destiny, Mustafa EL-Amin, New Mind Productions, Jersey City, NJ, 1988

Father and Son Relationship: Looking Towards The Future, Mustafa EL-Amin, EL-Amin Productions, Newark, NJ 1997

The Religion Of Islam, Maulana Ali Muhammad Book Crafters, Chelsea, MI 1990

What Every American Should Know About Al-Islam and The Muslims, Muhammad Armiya Nu'Man, New Mind Productions, Jersey City, NJ 1985

OTHER BOOKS BY MUSTAFA EL-AMIN

Let There Be Light

AL-Islam Christianity & Freemasonry

Abraham's Legacy: Ancient Wisdom and Modern Reality

Freemasonry Ancient Egypt and the Islamic Destiny

African American Freemasons: Why They Should Accept AL-Islam

The Religion Of Islam And The Nation Of Islam: What Is The Difference ?

Afrocentricity Malcolm X And AL-Islam

Father And Son Relationship: Looking Towards The Future